**DATE DUE**

# MUAY THAI

## KICKBOXING COMBAT

Garrison Wells

Lerner Publications Company • Minneapolis

Lerner Publications Company
A division of Lerner Publishing Group, Inc.
241 First Avenue North
Minneapolis, MN 55401 U.S.A.

Website address: www.lernerbooks.com

Content Consultant: Steve Milles, Muay Thai trainer and retired professional Thai boxer


Library of Congress Cataloging-in-Publication Data

Wells, Garrison.
    Muay Thai : kickboxing combat / by Garrison Wells.
        p.    cm. — (Martial arts sports zone)
    Includes index.
    ISBN 978–0–7613–8457–1 (lib. bdg. : alk. paper)
        1. Muay Thai—Juvenile literature. I. Title.
    GV1127.T45W45 2012
    796.815—dc23                              2011037346

Manufactured in the United States of America
1 – BC – 12/31/11

Photo Credits: Arthur Kwiatkowski/iStockphoto, 5; Tumar/Shutterstock Images, 6, 7; Patrick Aventurier/ Gamma-Rapho/Getty Images, 9; Bain News Service/Library of Congress, 10 (top); Sahamongkolfilm/ Photofest, 10 (bottom); Magnet Releasing/Everett Collection, 11; Globo/Getty Images, 12; Photofriday/ Shutterstock Images, 13, 28, 29 (top); Pedro Jorge Henriques Monteiro/Shutterstock Images, 15; Bjorn Svensson/Photolibrary, 16; Pornchai Kittiwongsakul/AFP/Getty Images, 17; Nicholas Piccillo/Shutterstock Images, 18; Gary M. Prior/Getty Images, 19; Joe Klamar/AFP/Getty Images, 20; Paula Bronstein/Getty Images, 21, 24; Nicky Zhang/ColorChinaPhoto/AP Images, 23; Esther Lin/Zuffa LLC/Getty Images, 25; Forest Woodward/iStockphoto, 26–27; Richard Arthur/Alamy, 29 (bottom)
Backgrounds: Aleksandar Velasevic/iStockphoto, Eduardo Miller/Shutterstock Images, Photogalia/ Shutterstock Images
Front cover: © Imago/ZUMA Press (main); © iStockphoto.com/Aleksandar Velasevic (background).
Main body text set in ITC Serif Gothic Std Bold 11/17.
Typeface provided by Adobe Systems.

# TABLE OF CONTENTS

# CHAPTER ONE

# OVERVIEW OF MUAY THAI

On the TV show *Sport Science, Hardest Kick*, the power of a Muay Thai kick was measured. Many wanted to know a kick's exact force. Muay Thai champion Melchor Menor was on the show. He splintered a baseball bat with a low kick rated at 1,000 pounds (454 kilograms) of force. This is the same force as a hyena's bite, which can easily crush bones. Menor's kick was the most powerful ever measured on the show.

## BUDDHIST INFLUENCE

Muay Thai comes from the Asian country of Thailand. The Thai people follow the Buddhist religion. Thai Buddhism is woven into some of Muay Thai's customs and beliefs. For example, the *prajioud* and *mongkhon* are the armband and headband that a fighter wears during a match. Before a fighter puts them on, a Buddhist monk blesses them.

A Muay Thai kick is capable of breaking bones.

## WHAT IS MUAY THAI?

Muay Thai is a stand-up form of self-defense. It is a mysterious fighting style to many Americans. But it is becoming more known as a powerful martial art and striking sport. Muay Thai is known for its attacks using knees, elbows, fists, and kicks. It is also called the Art of Eight Limbs because it uses so many body parts.

Boxers fight in a 2010 Muay Thai match in Minsk, Belarus.

Many professional fighters in mixed martial arts (MMA) use Muay Thai. The martial art helps them in their stand-up fighting. Wanderlei Silva and Ernesto Hoost are two MMA fighters with Muay Thai backgrounds. The fighters compete in MMA tournaments, such as the Ultimate Fighting Championship (UFC), K1, and Pride. Some MMA professionals travel to Thailand to learn from local masters of the sport.

## WHY STUDY MUAY THAI?

Muay Thai is a useful form of self-defense. But it also gets its boxers in great shape. Muay Thai helps students build self-esteem and self-discipline. The martial art also has a spiritual side, with ties to Buddhism. Students of Muay Thai come together as part of a family.

Many Muay Thai fighters pray before matches.

# CHAPTER TWO

# HISTORY AND CULTURE

**M**uay Thai is the national sport of Thailand. The martial art was first used more than 500 years ago as a form of wartime hand-to-hand fighting. At that time, people also fought with swords, spears, and bows and arrows. As time passed, the martial art split into two forms. One form—*krabi krabong*—used weapons. The other—the hand-to-hand form—became Muay Thai.

## SPREAD BY KINGS

Thailand is a monarchy, ruled by a king. Thai kings have been important to Muay Thai's growth. They practiced the martial art

### THE RING

MUAY THAI BOXERS FIGHT IN A SQUARE RING SIMILAR TO WHAT IS USED IN BOXING. THE RING IS EITHER 18 SQUARE FEET (1.7 SQUARE METERS), 22 SQUARE FEET (2.0 SQ. M.), OR 24 SQUARE FEET (2.2 SQ. M.). FOUR PARALLEL ROPES ARE STRUNG ALONG THE OUTSIDE OF THE RING. THESE HELP KEEP THE BOXERS FROM FALLING OUT. THE SURFACE OF THE RING IS RUBBER OR ANOTHER SOFT MATERIAL COVERED IN CANVAS. THE THICKNESS IS BETWEEN ABOUT 1 TO 2 INCHES (2.5 TO 5.1 CENTIMETERS).

Muay Thai is deeply rooted in Thai history and culture.

themselves and ordered its use by the military. The best fighters were invited to the royal palace to teach nobles and the royal family. In the 1500s, King Naresuan made Muay Thai part of military training. Naresuan was a great martial artist himself.

## BEGINNINGS OF A SPORT

Muay Thai's wartime beginnings made it a brutal sport. Early on, fighters sometimes died. Over time, Muay Thai became a two-person contest that took place in a square ring. Fighters prepared by wrapping their hands with rope. Then they stepped into the ring. They punched and kicked their way to wins. The fighters did not wear padding, and there were no time limits.

Muay Thai became even more popular in 1868 under King Rama V. Because of the king's interest in the martial art, it became a way to exercise. People began to train for recreation and self-defense. Matches were held in villages throughout the kingdom.

Every village had its champion. In run-down rings and gyms, young men fought for pride and a little bit of money. There was great honor for those who won. As the decades passed, Muay Thai became more popular within the country. It also spread to other nations.

## MUAY THAI AT THE MOVIES

Muay Thai has been featured in several movies. These include *Ong Bak: The Thai Warrior* (2003), *Ong Bak 2: The Beginning* (2008), and *Ong Bak 3: The Final Battle* (2010). All three movies star the

Tony Jaa in the original *Ong Bak*

JeeJa Yanin *(right)* in *Chocolate*

amazing Tony Jaa. His mastery of his sport is also featured in *The Protector* (2005). Jaa started studying Muay Thai at the age of 10.

Equally impressive is Jaa-trained Dan Chubong in *Born to Fight* (2004). In *Chocolate* (2008) JeeJa Yanin wows viewers with her fast, graceful Muay Thai moves.

## MUAY THAI DAY

One of the sport's first heroes is Nai Khanomtom. During a war in the 1760s, neighboring Burma took over Thailand. The Burmese captured Khanomtom, a Muay Thai powerhouse. The Burmese king forced him to fight during a festival in 1774. The fight pitted Thailand's top fighter against Burma's top fighter. Khanomtom won. The king wasn't happy, so he forced Nai to fight nine other Burmese fighters without rest. He beat them all. His victory is celebrated in Thailand each year on March 17 on Muay Thai Day.

Jose Aldo used Muay Thai to become the first UFC Featherweight Champion in 2010.

## MUAY THAI IN MMA

Muay Thai skills are used in almost every UFC or MMA tournament. It is a fighting base for MMA fighters Wanderlei Silva, Mauricio Rua, Gina Carano, and Jose Aldo. Fighters who compete in MMA generally use a main martial art for their strikes and kicks. They usually use another martial art style for their ground moves. For example, someone might use Muay Thai as the stand-up fighting style. He or she will use Brazilian jiujitsu as the ground game.

With its use of elbows, knees, kicks, and punches, Muay Thai gives MMA fighters a lot of weapons. They also like the clinches (close holds) that are another key Muay Thai set of moves.

Clinched Muay Thai fighters attempt to strike each other with elbows and knees. A referee (right) watches closely.

# CHAPTER THREE

# PRACTICING MUAY THAI

In Thailand, children start Muay Thai training as early as five or six years old. Muay Thai competitions begin a few years later. In the United States, training can begin at this young age as well. But competition usually begins when a fighter reaches the early to mid-twenties.

In Muay Thai, a fighter is called *nak muay Thai*. This means "Thai boxer" in the Thai language. The term *boxer* is also used in the United States and Britain. One of the great things about the sport is that no single body type is best suited for Muay Thai. The most important element is that the nak muay listens to the *kru*, or teacher. The nak muay also needs to be committed to the training. Having good form and speed are two keys to success.

## SAFETY

Fighters should know the sport's safety basics before they start training. The most important thing is for a student to study with a skilled kru. The teacher should also recognize that the safety of the fighter is more

Muay Thai fighters often wear pads on their hands and shins during practice to prevent injury.

important than winning fights. Fighters need to train smartly by eating properly and getting proper rest.

Amateur fighters may or may not wear headgear and shin guards. This depends on the class they fight in and their experience level. However, professional fighters wear very little protective gear. They put on gloves, a mouthpiece, and a groin protector. Headgear is not allowed.

A young fighter in Bangkok, Thailand, uses the heavy bag to strengthen his shins.

## TRAINING

Fighters train with some basic equipment. They wrap their hands and wrists with strips of cloth. Boxing or training-bag gloves go over the wraps. The wraps and the gloves protect the fighter's hands from injuries that can be caused by punching a heavy bag. Boxing gloves come in different weights, from 6 to 20 ounces (170 to 567 grams). Training-bag gloves are used for heavy-bag training. A third kind of glove is for grappling (wrestling on a mat). These gloves are used in MMA. They have thinner padding and open thumbs and palms so it is easier for a fighter to grab an opponent.

The heavy bags weigh 100 to 150 pounds (45 to 68 kg) and hang from the ceiling. A nak muay gets a good workout by punching and kicking a heavy bag. The bag never gets tired! This is why it is a great training tool. Bag work is usually done in rounds of three minutes with a one-minute rest. This is similar to a fight. Sometimes the training time is longer and the rest shorter.

In addition to training with bags, fighters practice with their trainers. Trainers wear focus mitts. These are targets that the fighter can throw punches at. Trainers also hold Thai pads near their bodies. They protect the trainer from the fighter's practice kicks, punches, knees, and elbows. Training with pads is supposed to be similar to a real fight without the potential for injury. Unlike many other martial arts, Muay Thai has no belts to show a fighter's skill level.

A trainer holds Thai pads while a fighter practices her kicks.

A fighter practices an elbow strike during training.

## FIGHTING MOVES

Muay Thai fighters have many moves to choose from in the ring. Elbows can be used in several directions. These include straight across, straight up, and backward. These strikes are used to finish an opponent or to take down the opponent with a slashing strike.

In Muay Thai, students are trained to hit with their shins instead of the foot. The foot has smaller bones and can be injured easily. The shin is stronger and more powerful. MMA fighters like the roundhouse kick because of its power. Its targets can be the leg, the side, the midsection, or the head. The kick's power comes from delivering it while turning the hips and entire body. MMA fighter Gabriel Gonzaga used a roundhouse kick to knock out Mirko Filipovic in UFC 70 in 2007.

## HARD TIMES

In ancient times, serious Muay Thai fighters were known to kick bamboo 1,000 times a day to harden their shins. The constant pounding damages the bones. They then harden as they heal, creating a harder surface for kicking.

Gabriel Gonzaga (left) knocked out Mirko Filipovic (right) with a roundhouse kick in 2007.

Italy's Alan Saitta *(left)* delivers a left long knee to Slovakia's Marcel Jáger *(right)* in a 2011 fight.

Muay Thai also uses several types of knee strikes. They include the straight knee, the horizontal knee, and the flying knee. These are very powerful and can cause knockouts. The jumping knee strike is when the fighter jumps up and strikes with the knee. For the flying knee, the boxer takes a step, then jumps and strikes with the opposite knee. Knee strikes are among the favorites of UFC champion Anderson Silva. He used them to help defeat Chris Leben in 2006.

Knees are also often used in the clinch. In this method, the fighter holds onto the opponent's neck. Then the fighter drives his or her knee upward into the opponent's head, face, and chest. For the front clinch, the fighter's hands are put behind the opponent's neck or back of the head. Pressure is put on the neck, with one palm placed on top of the other. From this position knees can be driven into the head while the head is pressed down into the strike.

For defense, Muay Thai includes blocking and striking with a foot jab. The foot jab controls distance between the opponents. These jabs are quick and powerful kicks used to keep the opponent off balance. Muay Thai experts create a wall of defense with their arms, legs, and shoulders.

A female fighter wears prajioud and performs ram muay before a fight.

## THE DANCE

BEFORE A FIGHT, FIGHTERS SOMETIMES PERFORM A DANCE CALLED WAI KHRU RAM MUAY OR RAM MUAY. IT'S A WAY TO SHOW RESPECT TO TEACHERS AND TRAINERS. FIGHTERS BOW TO HONOR THE BUDDHA, THE FOUNDER OF BUDDHISM. THE DANCE MAY BE PERFORMED TO TRADITIONAL THAI MUSIC. SOME FIGHTERS WEAR THE PRAJIOUD AND THE MONGKHON DURING THE CEREMONY. THE DANCE IS PERFORMED BEFORE FIGHTS ALL OVER THE WORLD.

# CHAPTER FOUR

# COMPETITION

Once a fighter has a solid background of fighting skills, he or she can start competing. Fights can feature local amateur athletes. Or fights can be international tournaments held in large stadiums and arenas. Large tournaments feature professional fighters from around the world. Two of the biggest events are the K1 in Japan and Battle in the Desert in Nevada.

## SUPER PUNCH

A popular Muay Thai move used in MMA includes the superman punch. It is also known as the cobra punch and the diving punch. To do the punch, the fighter brings a back leg forward and fakes a kick. Then the fighter snaps the leg back and throws a head punch. The motion creates a powerful punch because of the force of the body moving forward.

During competition, fighters do not wear shin protectors.

Most boxers in Thailand start fighting at the age of 13 or 14. They are retired by their mid- to late 20s. Thais are glued to their TV screens to watch the action and to make bets on the winner.

In the rest of the world, most professionals are in their 20s and 30s. Usually boxers are done fighting by their mid-thirties. Boxers often start fighting in small, local matches. Once they win, they start fighting in more publicized fights against bigger stars.

## WOMEN IN MUAY THAI

Women also train in Muay Thai. Many find the sport a good way to stay fit and strong. A growing number compete as well, although not as many as men. In Thailand the growth of women in the sport is slowed by traditional Thai superstition. It is said that women in the ring bring bad luck. Some women do still compete, though.

Top female fighters include Emily Bearden and Jeri Sitzes from the United States. Linda Ooms and Germaine de Randamie from the Netherlands are also good fighters. Julie Kitchen and Helene Garnett represent the best from Britain.

Women fighting in Thailand

Alistair Overeem (right)
knees Fabricio Werdum
(left) during an MMA fight
in 2011.

## MMA'S MUAY THAI STARS

Among fans, Muay Thai is best known for its wide use in MMA. Almost every MMA fighter uses at least some Muay Thai moves. In fact, schools of martial arts that offer grappling, such as Brazilian jiujitsu and sambo, often offer Muay Thai to round out training.

Muay Thai is popular in K1 tournaments in Japan, where it is often referred to as kickboxing. In 2010 the champion of the K1 World Grand Prix in Japan was Muay Thai star Alistair Overeem. Muay Thai is often seen in the UFC and other professional tours such as Strikeforce.

One of the most popular Muay Thai fighters of all time is Samart Payakaroon. Payakaroon was both a Muay Thai champion and Junior Featherweight world boxing champion. He was known for his smart movement in the ring. He retired in the early 1990s. Current greats include Yodsanklai Fairtex and Buakaw Por Pramuk. Fairtex is known for his near-perfect fighting technique. A Thai newspaper called him the Boxing Computer. Pramuk won K1 World MAX championships in 2004 and 2006.

## THE IMPORTANCE OF LEG KICKS

Kicks to the leg may not seem too dangerous. But fighters have defeated their opponents with low kicks. These kicks target the thigh above the knee and weaken the leg. It is very painful and has led to some fights being stopped due to injury. Ernesto Hoost used the low kick to stop Mirko Filipovic in a K1 tournament in Japan.

MMA fighter Marco Ruas has trained in Muay Thai. He is the former UFC light heavyweight champion. He is also the winner of the 2005 Middleweight Pride Grand Prix in Japan.

## A WELL-ROUNDED MARTIAL ART

The names of professional fighters who train in Muay Thai speak volumes. Muay Thai is an effective martial art loaded with benefits. If a person is wanting to practice self-defense, Muay Thai has what it takes. If looking for sport, Muay Thai can lead the way to great fighting competitions. Either way, a person cannot lose by practicing Muay Thai.

Two boxers practice in a park in London, England.

### INCREASED POPULARITY

MMA AND UFC TOURNAMENTS HAVE INCREASED THE POPULARITY OF MUAY THAI MANY TIMES OVER. THE ONCE LARGELY UNKNOWN MARTIAL ART HAS HUNDREDS OF THOUSANDS OF MMA FANS. ONCE RUN-DOWN SCHOOLS IN THAILAND HAVE BECOME TOP MMA TRAINING CENTERS.

# TECHNIQUES
# HOW-TO

## ELBOW STRIKE

A fighter drives the back leg into the floor and stands tall. The fighter bends the arm and swings the point of the elbow into the opponent. The elbow can be swung up, down, or across the fighter's body.

A front kick

## FRONT KICK

A fighter stands on one leg and draws the knee of the other leg high toward the chest. Then the fighter extends the leg out from the hip and hits the opponent with the ball of the foot, striking either the head or the body.

## SIDE CLINCH

A fighter passes one arm around the front of the opponent with the fighter's shoulder pressed into the opponent's armpit. The fighter passes the other arm around the opponent's back. This allows the fighter to apply knee strikes to the opponent's back or to easily throw the opponent.

## ROUNDHOUSE KICK

A fighter rotates on the ball of the foot of the supporting leg and turns the entire body to strike with the shin of the impacting leg. Targets may be the opponent's thigh, midsection, or head. There are many variations of this kick—jumping and spinning can be added—but all build on these basics.

# GLOSSARY

**AMATEUR**

an activity done for fun without expectation of payment

**BUDDHISM**

a religion that originated in Asia and that millions of people, including most Thais, follow

**CLINCH**

a move that locks two fighters in close quarters

**GRAPPLING**

wrestling on the mat

**MONARCHY**

a country ruled by a king or a queen

**NOBLES**

people who were a part of a high social class by birth

**PROFESSIONAL**

something done as a job for payment

**STRIKE**

a hit on an opponent

**SUPERSTITION**

a belief stemming from fear that some action will influence the outcome of an event

# FOR MORE INFORMATION

## FURTHER READING

Delp, Christoph. *Muay Thai Basics: Introductory Thai Boxing Techniques.* Berkeley, CA: Blue Snake Books, 2005.

Donaldson, Madeline. *Thailand.* Minneapolis: Lerner Publications Company, 2011.

Krauss, Erich. *Muay Thai Unleashed: Learn Technique and Strategy from Thailand's Warrior Elite.* New York: McGraw-Hill, 2006.

## WEBSITES

### International Federation of Muaythai Amateur
**http://www.ifmamuaythai.org**
The website of the world governing body of amateur Muay Thai features articles and news about amateur competition, as well as information on past and upcoming tournaments.

### U.S. Muay Thai Association
**http://www.usmta.com**
This website includes information about Muay Thai schools, instructors, and events across the United States.

### World Muaythai Council
**http://www.wmcmuaythai.org**
The website for the world governing body of professional Muay Thai features the history, rules, and news of the sport.

# INDEX

## ABOUT THE AUTHOR

Garrison Wells is a third-degree black belt in Nihon jujitsu, a first-degree black belt in judo, a third-degree black belt in Goju-ryu karate, and a first-degree black belt in kobudo. He is also an award-winning journalist and writer. Wells lives in Colorado.